20-in-10

Linking Music and Literacy with Twenty,
Ten-Minute Mini-Lessons
and Activities for Primary Learners

20-in-10

Linking Music and Literacy with
Twenty, Ten-Minute Mini-Lessons
and Activities for Primary Learners

Luana Mitten

Music
by
Cathy Fink and Marcy Marxer

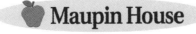 Maupin House

20-in-10: Linking Music and Literacy with Twenty, Ten-Minute
Mini-Lessons and Activities for Primary Learners
by Luana Mitten

Cover Design and Book Layout: Mickey Cuthbertson
Illustrations: Josh Clark
Editor: Erica Dix

Lesson concepts and ideas for "When the Rain Comes Down," "It's a Shame," "A Ballet
Dancing Truck Driver," "Grandpa's Farm," and "The Cowpoke Dance" contributed by
Cathy Fink & Marcy Marxer.

Library of Congress Cataloging-in-Publication Data
Mitten, Luana K.
20-in-10 : linking music and literacy with twenty, ten-minute mini-lessons and activities for primary learners /
Luana Mitten ; music and lyrics by Cathy Fink and Marcy Marxer.
    p. cm.
Includes bibliographical references (p.   ).
ISBN 0-929895-86-X
1. School music--Instruction and study. 2. Interdisciplinary approach in education. 3. Reading (Primary) I.
Title: Twenty in ten. II. Title: Linking music and literacy with twenty, ten-minute mini-lessons. III. Fink, Cathy.
IV. Marxer, Marcy. V. Title.
MT930.M66 2005
372.87'044--dc22

                        2005009702

Photo of Cathy Fink & Marcy Marxer courtesy of Dane Penland.
To book Cathy Fink & Marcy Marxer for conferences and performances
visit www.cathymarcy.com

"Hello, Hello, Hello" © 1989 Marcy Marxer
"There's a Fairy in My Pocket" © 2001 Marcy Marxer
"The Rhythm of the World" © 2001 Cathy Fink
"Grandpa's Farm" © 1986 Marcy Marxer
"The Alphabet Boogie" © 1987 Cathy Fink and Marcy Marxer
"When the Rain Comes Down" © 1977 Bob Devlin
"A Ballet Dancing Truck Driver" © 1996 Marcy Marxer
"It's a Shame" © 1984 Cathy Fink & Marcy Marxer
"Goodnight, Goodnight" © 1991 Cathy Fink
"The Jazzy Three Bears" © 1984 Cathy Fink
"The Cowpoke Dance" © 1986 Marcy Marxer
The songs on this collection have been licensed from several of Cathy & Marcy's
different recordings on Rounder Records.

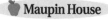 Maupin House

Visit *www.maupinhouse.com* for lyrics to Cathy Fink & Marcy Marxer songs
Maupin House Publishing, Inc.   800-524-0634 • 352-373-5588
PO Box 90148 • Gainesville, FL 32607   (fax) 352-373-5546
www.maupinhouse.com   (email) info@maupinhouse.com
Publishing Professional Resources that Improve Classroom Performance

Printed in China through Prolong, Hong Kong
ISBN-10: 0-929895-86-X, ISBN-13: 978-0-929895864

Dedication

To my parents, Marvin and Jean Robertson

~LKM

Table of Contents

Preface

Music and literacy go hand in hand. With no formal training in music, children learn their ABCs with a simple song. They learn about counting, rhythm, rhyme, call and response, auditory recognition, focus, sequencing, memorization, and so much more. The boredom of repetition disappears with a song, melody, or rhythm, which makes music a perfect medium for teaching nearly everything.

As musicians, we are inspired to apply our songwriting, performance, and musical productions to helping children learn life skills. We have discovered how to do this intuitively, as frequent guests in classrooms and in libraries, as performers in concert halls and festivals, and as godparents and aunts. In the process, we have been able to help classroom teachers find more ways to use music without feeling like they need to be maestros. A little rhythm goes a long way!

We have found that songs can inspire days and weeks of exploration and expansion. One day you listen, another day you sing along, and another you identify something in the song that ties into a new skill or lesson.

20-in-10 offers a delightful series of "mini-teaching moments" that both students and teachers can look forward to. The more fun we make it, the more children will want to learn. The songs and lessons in this book are meant to be easy, accessible, and quick for teachers while offering challenges for young learners in the positive context of music. Finished with math ten minutes before recess? Try a mini-teaching moment with music. Do you have a new reading-skills lesson? See if there's a song on the CD or a lesson that fits into your curriculum.

Creative teachers can easily expand these twenty lessons into their own mini-teaching moments. We are excited to join Maupin House for this new approach to teaching literacy skills.

Cathy Fink & Marcy Marxer

Introduction
The Power of Connecting Music and Early Literacy

Music is powerful. Ask any adult to describe something they remember from their early elementary days and most will speak of a memory tied to music. In *Arts with the Brain in Mind*, Eric Jensen writes that music "works to aid our memory because the beat, the melody, and the harmonies serve as 'carriers' for the semantic content. That's why it's easier to recall the words to a song than a conversation. Put key words to music, and you will typically get better recall" (41-42).

Despite its proven success in increasing memory retention and facilitating conceptual learning, music is often absent from today's classrooms, where state assessments are priority. Teachers who feel pressured to teach to the standards often find they have little time for integrating music into their curriculum. In fact, many consider music "fluff" that must be sacrificed to make time for more academic subjects.

20-in-10 uniquely addresses the realities of today's classroom by introducing music as a powerful ally to your early literacy instruction. The songs and lessons in this book allow you to use high-quality children's music for short "mini-teaching moments" during those otherwise wasted minutes of empty class time, such as first thing in the morning, before or after lunch, during transition times, or at the end of the teaching day. When you integrate music and literacy you create an environment that fosters alert, active, and engaged young minds.

Using *20-in-10* in Your Classroom

Before beginning the lessons, relax and enjoy the music with your class. Like any other literature model that you use for reading or writing instruction, students should be familiar with and enjoy the music before it is used for an instructional purpose.

A *20-in-10* mini-lesson takes about ten minutes to do and can be used at any time during the day. In fact, the lessons work best if they are interspersed throughout your day and not clumped together. Because each lesson is designed to be flexible, you can cut or expand it to fit your schedule. Here are some suggested ways to include them:

- *20-in-10* mini-lessons make excellent transitions between activities, especially when you need to shift the energy level in your classroom. Use active, high-energy songs such as "The Cowpoke Dance" to help children get the wiggles out, or peaceful, calming songs like "When the Rain Comes Down" to segue from high-energy activities to more subdued, quiet tasks.
- The music is an effective warm-up to any task involving creativity or problem solving.
- *20-in-10* mini-lessons are an engaging way to introduce larger literacy lessons and illustrate how rhyming words and descriptive attributes can be used to review content and writing skills.
- The songs can serve as musical signals for daily routines like clean-up, which will help children gauge how much time they have to complete a task and prepare for the next activity.

The twenty mini-lessons in this book reflect a range of skills and concepts appropriate for primary students and can be done in any sequence. Keep in mind that you can modify the lessons to fit your students' instructional level.

Zipper Songs

Many of the songs in *20-in-10* are called "zipper songs." The term, which was first used by Lee Hays of the folk group The Weavers, refers to any song with a word or line that easily "zips out" to make room for a new word, line, or verse that can be "zipped in." An obvious example is "Old MacDonald Had a Farm." You zip *out* an animal and its sound and zip *in* a different animal and its sound.

Primary students love zipper songs, as integrating them across the curriculum makes learning fun and effective. You can sing the zipper songs a cappella without the CD, or you can leave the CD on and lower the volume to help students carry the tune and easily sing their own words.

The zipper icon will indicate the following zipper songs:

"Hello, Hello, Hello"
"There's a Fairy in My Pocket"
"Grandpa's Farm"
"When the Rain Comes Down"
"A Ballet Dancing Truck Driver"
"It's a Shame"
"Goodnight, Goodnight"

20-in-10 and Literacy Instruction

20-in-10 offers many ways to enhance literacy instruction in your primary classroom. Try some of the ideas listed below to get started. You'll discover many more as you use the songs and mini-lessons.

Reading

- Use the lyrics to develop students' vocabulary. Ask students what "great" means when used in the comparison "great and small" in "When the Rain Comes Down" or what the word "shame" means in the song "It's a Shame." These types of discussions allow students to practice inference skills that will help them learn new meanings for words, and because the words are used in a song, they will remember the meanings.

- Create class big books for each song. Type out the lyrics by verse, printing each verse on a separate page, and have your students illustrate the verses. Then use these class-made big books in literacy centers, as a big book for shared reading, or when singing the songs together.

- When you introduce a new song, copy the song lyrics from the book for each student to put in their poetry notebook. Reading lyrics during independent reading builds fluency. You can also print out lyrics online at **www.maupinhouse.com.**

- Use song lyrics as a base for class phonics or word study (chunking, rhyming, alliteration) work charts. Make sure charts are accessible for students to reference during reading and writing activities.
- Song lyrics will also develop students' listening skills and their ability to visualize.

Writing

- Research has discovered that listening to music before writing has a positive effect on two key cognitive systems used in writing: creativity and problem solving (Jensen 2001). Use a *20-in-10* mini-lesson to begin a writing workshop and provide a quick oral review of a previously-taught writing-craft skill.
- Song lyrics provide excellent practice of Target Skills™, or specific, single-skill writing-craft techniques and conventions. Zipper songs also offer a wonderful support for students as they try out new writing-craft skills orally or in writing. One way to do this is to make a blackline master of the lyrics, omitting the zipper words and leaving a blank for students to fill in the missing word or words. Using "Grandpa's Farm" as a model for practicing descriptive attributes works well. See the Appendix for a descriptive attribute chart.

Kindergarten Blackline Master Example

Down on Grandpa's farm there is a (descriptive attribute) (object name).

First and Second Grade Blackline Master Example

Down on Grandpa's farm there is a (descriptive attribute) (object name). The (repeat object name), it goes a lot like this: (sound).

For example: Down on Grandpa's farm there is a galloping horse.

Look for the **⑨ TARGET SKILLS™** icon when seeking out lessons that focus on a specific writing-craft skill.

The chart that follows links Target Skills with songs that can be used as models for teaching specific writing-craft techniques.

Writing-Craft Target Skills™

Song	Descriptive Attributes	Strong Verbs	Alliteration, Rhyming	Onomatopoeia	Specificity	Speak directly to reader	Comparisons	Supporting details
"Hello, Hello, Hello"					✔	✔		
"There's a Fairy in My Pocket"	✔	✔	✔					
"The Rhythm of the World"		✔	✔			✔		
"Grandpa's Farm"	✔			✔				
"The Alphabet Boogie"		✔	✔			✔		
"When the Rain Comes Down"	✔	✔				✔	✔	
"A Ballet Dancing Truck Driver"		✔		✔				✔
"It's a Shame"			✔			✔		
"Goodnight, Goodnight"	✔	✔	✔					
"The Jazzy Three Bears"	✔	✔	✔					
"The Cowpoke Dance"	✔	✔				✔		

Whether you use these mini-lessons to model reading comprehension and writing-craft skills or to occupy those little awkward gaps of time throughout your teaching day, you'll note the powerful, positive impact music has on learning. Allow the songs in *20-in-10* to show you and your students the creative and instructional value of bringing music into the classroom!

song **1**

"Hello, Hello, Hello"
© Marcy Marxer, 2 Spoons Music,
ASCAP, 1989

Hello, hello, hello (2X)
Boys and girls around the world say
Hello, hello, hello.

Hello, hello, hello (2X)
Hey, have you heard? What's the
word? It's Hello, Hello, Hello.

Mile after mile,
from Hartford to L.A.,
A wave and a smile and
this is what we say:

Hello, hello, hello (2X)
Let's have some fun. You're the one!
Hello, hello, hello.

Hola, Hola (2X)
Boys and girls in Mexico say
Hola, Hola.

Hola, Hola (2X)
To say "hello" los niños* say
Hola, Hola.

Mile after mile,
from Cordoba to Monterey,
A wave and a smile
and this is what we say:

Hola, Hola (2X)
Let's have some fun. You're the one!
Hola, hola.

Hello, Hello, Hello

"Hello, Hello, Hello" is a perfect morning-gathering and greeting song. Because it builds awareness of different cultures and languages, it is a nice introduction to social studies, geography, and even basic social skills.

Lesson 1.1
Skill/Concept: Social Skills, Movement

Materials:  CD set to track 1

► Chart paper

- Discuss the different ways people "talk" to each other without saying a word by using body language. Questions to ask: "Who can demonstrate one way to say hello without using any words? Can anyone think of another way we greet people without words?" Continue eliciting responses and allow students to practice different actions until they run out of ideas. Write each suggestion on chart paper and draw quick sketches of stick figures demonstrating the different non-verbal greetings.

- Select one non-verbal greeting from the list and ask the students to greet their neighbor(s) with this gesture each time they sing the words "hello, hello, hello." Now play "Hello, Hello, Hello."

- Children will enjoy selecting different non-verbal greetings from the class list each day.

- Over the next several days add new greetings to the class chart. Discuss the differences between each greeting and its usage, as well as the ways in which greetings may change depending on who we are greeting. Questions to ask: "Show me an appropriate gesture you could use to greet the principal. How is it different from a non-verbal greeting you would use to say hello to a friend?"

Wave

Shake hands

Namaste, Namaste
Boys and girls in India say
Namaste.

Namaste, Namaste
To say "hello" the bacha* say
Namaste.

Mile after mile,
from Madras to Bombay,
A wave and a smile and
this is what we say:

Namaste, Namaste
Let's have some fun. You're the one!
Namaste.

Jambo-sana, Jambo-sana
Boys and girls in Africa say
Jambo-sana.

Jambo-sana, Jambo-sana
To say "hello" the watoto* say
Jambo-sana.

Mile after mile,
from Nairobi to Mbale,
A wave and a smile and
this is what we say:

Jambo-sana, Jambo-sana
Let's have some fun. You're the one!
Jambo-sana.

Hola! Jambo-sana! Namaste!
Hello, Hello, Hello!

* "niños," "bacha," and "watoto"
mean "children"

Bow

Kiss

Hug

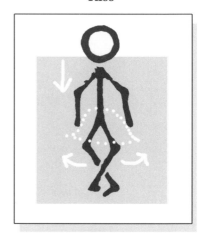

Curtsey

Smile and nod head

High-five

Lesson 1.2

Skill/Concept: Social Studies, Map Skills, Cultural Awareness

Materials:  CD set to track 1
- ► World Map
- ► Pointer
- ► Stickers

- Sing "Hello, Hello, Hello" with the class. Ask students to recall the name of each country identified in the song. List each country on the board.

- Using a world map, help students locate each country named in "Hello, Hello, Hello." As the children locate each country, label it with a sticker so they can easily find it again each time they sing the song. Children-of-the-world stickers or colored star stickers work well. Older students will also enjoy locating the cities named in each country.

- Now play "Hello, Hello, Hello" again. This time, ask one child to point to each country on the map while the class sings. Be sure to have the world map with stickers available each time the class sings "Hello, Hello, Hello."

- Once students are familiar with the location of the countries, zip in new countries, cities, and languages for them to learn. Consider selecting new countries that reflect your students' diverse cultural backgrounds, countries currently in the news, or countries students are researching.

Suggested Books

Rabe, Tish. *There's a Map on My Lap! All About Maps*. New York: Random House, 2002.

Sweeney, Joan. *Me on the Map*. New York: Crown, 1996.

song 2

There's a fairy in my pocket.
I found her there one day.
She looked at me and
smiled and winked,
And then she said, "Let's play!"

There's a fairy in my pocket
And she's meant for only me.
And when the clock
strikes two o'clock
You'll find us having tea.

She has two bright red pigtails
And two tiny sparkly wings,
She sailed here in a nutshell
From a land of Queens and Kings.

There's a fairy in my pocket
And she's wearing purple socks,
And when my pocket's full I know
She's been collecting rocks.

There's a fairy in my pocket
And she has a tiny shirt.
And in her tiny pocket
Is a crystal and some dirt.

It's where she plants her garden
From the tiniest of seeds,
And one small drop of water
Is just what the garden needs.

There's a fairy in my pocket
And my pocket is a mess.
She leaves her laundry in a heap
And concentrates on chess.

There's a fairy in my pocket,
She hiccups and she slurps,
And people often look at me
And giggle when she burps.

There's a Fairy in My Pocket

"There's a Fairy in My Pocket" is rich in verse and imagination. This delightful oral story develops listening and visualization skills while helping you transition students from active to more quiet times throughout the day.

Lesson 2.1

Skill/Concept: Listening, Visualizing

Materials: CD set to track 2
► Paper and crayons

- Use "There's a Fairy in My Pocket" as a transition activity for several days before beginning to use it in instruction.

- Read the poem to your class without the CD. Use a bell to make a fairy-esque sound between each verse and have the children say the phrase "there's a fairy in my pocket." Encourage students to close their eyes as they listen to the poem and imagine what the child and her fairy friend are up to.

- When you've finished reading, ask students to quickly sketch one thing they visualized while listening to "There's a Fairy in My Pocket." Or provide students with a party-sized cup of play dough and have them make quick sculptures of one thing they visualized.

- When your students are finished, allow volunteers to share their sketches or sculptures.

- Repeat this activity several times throughout the school year, encouraging students to sketch or sculpt something new each time.

Lesson 2.2  TARGET SKILLS™

Skill/Concept: Descriptive Attributes, Strong Verbs

Materials: ⟨ CD set to track 2 ⟩
► Chart paper
► Descriptive attribute chart

- Once students have heard "There's a Fairy in My Pocket" several times as an oral story, use it to teach descriptive attributes. Review descriptive attributes (see Appendix) and ask your students to listen for them as you read the lyrics aloud. Students can signal a thumbs-up every time they hear a descriptive attribute.

- Next, ask students to list and label the descriptive attributes they heard in "There's a Fairy in My Pocket." Write down all the words they remembered on a class chart. For example:

Descriptive Attribute	Example from Story
number	two
color	bright red

She has a little fairy dog.
She named her small dog Clover.
For clovers can be magical,
Why would she call him Rover?

There's a fairy in my pocket
And she sings the sweetest song,
And when I hear her singing
I can't help but sing along.

She unfortunately loves to dance.
I wish she would abstain.
For dancing in my pocket
Isn't easy to explain.

There's a fairy in my pocket.
I am never quite alone.
She stays up 'til all hours
Chatting on the telephone.

She's chatting with her fairy friends,
The ones who stow away
In other people's pockets.
Some are near, some far away.

There's a fairy in my pocket,
She says she likes me best.
I don't believe I'll question her
Or put her to a test.

You see we two are
best of friends,
My fairy friend and I.
We play a game of tag
And then we share a piece of pie.

And when it's time to go to sleep
She lays upon my bed
With a feather for a blanket
And a wish under her head.

And when I get my story
And my little kiss goodnight,
My fairy lays beside me
And we sleep away the night.

- Because "There's a Fairy in My Pocket" is loaded with descriptive attributes, it will take a few days to list them all. Each day quickly review the attributes your students have discovered. Then challenge them to listen again for any new attributes.

- Repeat this same process for strong verbs that show action.

- Encourage students to practice using descriptive attributes and strong verbs by instructing them to zip new words into the song, "There's a_____ in my _____." Many students will stick with a fairy, but others may choose to have a "bug in their backpack," a "bear in their bed," or anything else they can think of. Be sure and model some examples so they understand the task.

NOTE: You may need to pause the CD after each verse to allow younger children more time to list attributes on the class chart. Older children may find it helpful to write down the words as they listen.

Suggested Books

Dubois, Pierre. *The Great Encyclopedia of Faeries.* London: Pavilion, 1999.

Froud, Brian. *Good Faeries.* New York: Simon & Schuster, 1998.

song **3**

The Rhythm of the World

"The Rhythm of the World" has a warm, peaceful rhythm. Children really enjoy using shakers, drums, and other rhythm instruments when they sing or hear this song.

TEACHER TIP: For an easy way to make plastic shakers, just fill plastic film canisters with rice, dried beans, sand, or rock salt and then seal the lids with hot glue. You'll notice that different ingredients yield slightly different sounds. These shakers can be used throughout the day and are especially effective during shared reading to help children hear the rhythm of language.

Lesson 3.1
Skill/Concept: Earth's Rotation, Calendar, Rhythm

Materials:  CD set to track 3

- Provide students with rhythm instruments or shakers to use while singing "The Rhythm of the World." Then sing the song as a lead-in to science lessons or calendar activities.
- At the end of the song, take a mini-teaching moment to discuss one or more of the following concepts:
    1. What constitutes one day?
    2. Describe a 24-hour timeline.
    3. What constitutes one year?

Chorus:
Ching-a-ling-a-ling,
hear the bells ring.
Ching-a-ling-a-long, sing a song.
Ching-a-ling-a-lum,
hands on a drum.
That is the rhythm of the world, oh
That is the rhythm of the world.

Oh the sun comes up and we say hello
To the birds and the sky and the people we know.
All day long we work and play
Thanks to the sun shining on our day.

Chorus

Oh the planet earth goes
around the sun,
It takes a year till the journey's done.
Night and day, the earth will spin
Until your birthday comes again.

Chorus

Oh the moon goes around the
earth that way,
As the planets circle their time away.
The stars keep dancing in the sky
To tell their tales to you and I.

Chorus

When the sun goes down and we
stretch and yawn,
The moon slides up as the
nighttime comes,
The stars come out to
sprinkle the sky
With dreams of another day gone by.

Chorus (2X)

4. How does the earth rotate?
5. Does the moon rotate?
6. Challenge students to calculate and chart their ages in years and months.
7. What is the difference between a calendar year (January to December) and the year between two birthdays?

Lesson 3.2 🌀 **TARGET SKILLS™**

Skill/Concept: Rhyming Words, Listening

Materials: ◉ ▬ CD set to track 3 ▬
► Chart paper

- Review familiar rhyming word pairs with your students before playing "The Rhythm of the World." Then ask students to listen for more rhyming words as they sing the song.

- After singing "The Rhythm of the World," challenge students to name any rhyming pairs they heard. Write the pairs on chart paper in columns. Ask students to brainstorm other words that rhyme with any of the rhyming pairs on the chart, and circle the letters that make the rhyming sounds.

- Keep this chart accessible and continue adding rhyming words to it over the next several days. Review the rhyming pairs already on the list and encourage students to listen carefully for new rhyming pairs.

NOTE: Depending on your students' instructional level, you may need to pause the CD at the end of each verse and list the rhyming pairs.

As a follow-up activity have students brainstorm different types of cycles:

Cycles in nature: the seasons, life cycles of plants
Cycles in their lives: washing clothes, doing chores, weekly schedules
Silly cycles: shoes tied, shoes untied

song **4**

Grandpa's Farm

You may be tempted to save "Grandpa's Farm" for use during a unit on farms. Resist the temptation! "Grandpa's Farm" provides an excellent opportunity for children to make the connection between a writer's use of descriptive attributes and a reader or listener's ability to visualize. It also allows students to practice working with descriptive attributes as they zip new characters, settings, and supporting details into the song.

Lesson 4.1 ⊙ **TARGET SKILLS™**

Skill/Concept: Visualizing, Descriptive Attributes, Listening

Materials: 🔘 CD set to track 4
► Unlined paper on clipboards
► Crayons

NOTE: As mentioned in the introduction, it's generally wise for students to be familiar with the lyrics and the tune of a song before they participate in any directed learning activity based on it. This mini-lesson is an exception, as it is most effective for students to do the activity while they listen to "Grandpa's Farm" for the first time.

- Before playing "Grandpa's Farm," talk with your students about how writers use descriptive attributes to help us, the

"Grandpa's Farm"
Traditional, arrangement
© Marcy Marxer, 2 Spoons Music, ASCAP, 1986

Down on Grandpa's farm there is a big brown cow (2X)
The cow, it goes a lot like this:
<u>moo</u> (2X)

Chorus:
We're on our way, we're on our way
On our way to Grandpa's farm (2X)

Down on Grandpa's farm there is a little white chicken (2X)
The chicken, it goes a lot like this:
<u>bok, bok</u> (2X)

Chorus

Down on Grandpa's farm there is a little spotted goat (2X)
The goat, it goes a lot like this:
<u>baaah, baaah</u> (2X)

Chorus

Down on Grandpa's farm there is an old banjo (2X)
The banjo, it goes a lot like this:
<u>pluck, pluck</u> (2X)

Chorus (2X)

reader/listener, picture what they are describing. Tell them this is called "visualizing." Demonstrate this concept by asking students to close their eyes and listen as you describe something, such as your family pet. Tell them to keep their eyes closed until they can "see" in their minds what you are describing. Students can open their eyes as soon as they have visualized the thing you depicted.

- Tell students they are going to listen to a song called "Grandpa's Farm." Ask them to close their eyes and visualize each thing described on the farm.

- When the song is over, call on a several students to describe what they imagined on the farm.

- On another day play "Grandpa's Farm" again, asking students to sketch one thing they visualized on Grandpa's farm.

- Provide each child with a blank sheet of paper and crayons before starting the CD. Remind children that closing their eyes as they listen might help them "see" the pictures in their heads. Once the song is over, give students time to complete their sketches and share them with the class. You'll find that their visualizations will improve the more they practice.

NOTE: It is important to remind children that there are no right or wrong visualizations.

Lesson 4.2 TARGET SKILLS™

Skill/Concept: Descriptive Attributes, Onomatopoeia

Materials: CD set to track 4
► Chart paper
► Descriptive attribute chart

- Before playing "Grandpa's Farm," quickly review descriptive attributes (see Appendix). Questions to ask: "Who can tell me what a descriptive attribute is? Why do writers use descriptive attributes? Can you give me some examples of descriptive attributes?"

- Now play "Grandpa's Farm" and have students close their eyes and listen for descriptive attributes such as color, size, and special features.

- At the end of "Grandpa's Farm," ask the students to think about what they visualized as they listened to the song. Make a list of each object and the corresponding descriptive attributes. Once you've made this list, have students zip new settings, characters, descriptive attributes, and sounds into the song. For example:

  1. Setting: "Down at <u>Grandma's Zoo</u> . . ."
  2. Characters: "there is a big brown <u>bear</u>. The <u>bear</u>, it goes a lot like this: <u>growl</u>."
  3. Descriptive attributes: "there is a <u>baby white cow</u>. The cow, it goes a lot like this: <u>moo</u>."
  4. Characters and descriptive attributes: "there is a <u>mean gray wolf</u>. The wolf, it goes a lot like this: <u>howl</u>."

- Each time you revisit "Grandpa's Farm" allow students to practice zipping in new characters, settings, and/or descriptive attributes. Then have one student write out and illustrate the new verses. Compile these into a class book.

NOTE: Don't forget to add these examples to your class descriptive attribute big book or chart!

Suggested Books
Fleming, Denise. *Barnyard Banter*. New York: Holt, 1994.

Fox, Mem. *Hattie and the Fox*. New York: Bradbury Press, 1986.

Suggested Books on Visualizing
Shaw, Charles G. *It Looked Like Spilt Milk*. New York: Harper, 1947.

The Alphabet Boogie

"The Alphabet Boogie"
© Cathy Fink & Marcy Marxer,
Leading Role Music, ASCAP, 1987

There's a letter in my cereal,
a letter in my soup.
A letter on the wall that
makes me loop de loop.
A letter on my shirt,
a letter on my socks.
And all of these letters
make me want to rock

To the alphabet boogie
On the radio.
It's the alphabet boogie—one, two,
three let's go!
ABCDEFG HIJKLMNOP
QRSTUV WXYZ

It's the alphabet boogie
On the radio.
It's the alphabet boogie—one, two,
three let's go!

Now the alphabet boogie
is an easy dance.
Anyone can do it if they
have the chance.
It starts with your toes
and it moves on up,
Just think of those letters as you
dance and jump

The "The Alphabet Boogie" works well as a transition from one activity to another or as an introduction to reading, writing, phonics, and word study activities. Allowing students to sing along and boogie with the beat helps them get the wiggles out and prepare to focus during instruction.

Lesson 5.1

Skill/Concept: Letter Identification, One-to-One Matching

Materials:  CD set to track 5

► ABC Chart (wall mount or poster)
► Pointer

- Ask a student to use a pointer and point to each letter on the class ABC chart as your class sings along with "The Alphabet Boogie."

- At the end of the song, ask the same student to use the pointer again, this time pointing to each letter on the ABC chart while the class reads the alphabet from A to Z. (Remember, the emphasis is on one-to-one matching.)

- Now select a second child to use the pointer and listen to the "The Alphabet Boogie" a second time.

- After the second time through, challenge

your class to read the alphabet *backwards* as the student points to the ABC chart from Z to A.

- Once students have become experts at saying the alphabet forwards and backwards, try some of the following suggestions to challenge them and test their one-to-one matching skills.

  1. Ask individuals or small groups to read the alphabet forwards and backwards.
  2. Have students read the alphabet saying every other letter.
  Example: A, C, E, G . . . or B, D, F, H . . .

  This can also be done backwards for an additional challenge.
  Example: Z, X, V, T . . . or Y, W, U, S . . .

  3. Divide the students into two groups—boys versus girls works well. As you point to the ABC chart, have each group read every other letter.
  Example: Girls *A*, Boys *B*, Girls *C*, Boys *D* . . .

  Naming every other letter backwards provides an additional challenge.
  Example: Girls *Z*, Boys *Y*, Girls *X*, Boys *W* . . .

To the alphabet boogie
On the radio.
It's the alphabet boogie—one, two, three let's go!
ABCDEFG HIJKLMNOP
QRSTUV WXYZ

It's the alphabet boogie
On the radio.
It's the alphabet boogie—one, two three let's go!

There's an old man lives in our town,
He can boogie up
and he can boogie down.
But the funniest thing
that man can do
Is the alphabet backwards,
hey, can you?

Sing the alphabet backwards
On the radio.
It's the alphabet backwards—three, two, one let's go!
ZYXWVUT SRQPONML
KJIHGFE DCBA

It's the alphabet boogie
On the radio.
It's the alphabet boogie—one, two, three let's go! (2X)

The Alphabet Boogie 19

Lesson 5.2  TARGET SKILLS™

Skill/Concept: Letter Sounds, One-to-One Matching, Alliteration

Materials: CD set to track 5
► ABC Chart (wall mount or poster)
► Pointer

- Play the "The Alphabet Boogie" before a quick review of letter sounds or as an introduction to a phonics mini-lesson.

- After singing the song together, review various letters and the sounds they make. Then select a focus sound. Focus sounds can be made with individual letters or chunks of letters. Have your students brainstorm a list of words containing the focus sound and write each word on chart paper. After listing several words, have students circle the letter(s) that make the focus sound in each word. Keep these charts accessible during reading and writing activities so students can refer to them.

- Older children can practice alliteration by brainstorming several words that begin with a focus sound and stringing those words together in silly sentences.

- "The Alphabet Boogie" can serve as a springboard for phonics lessons as well as letter-and word-study activities throughout the school year. Here are several possibilities for different charts you can create:

Chart 1
Sounds that are made by one letter located at the beginning of a word.

Words beginning with /b/

bat	ball
bike	boat
bell	book
bee	bug

Chart 2

Sounds that are made by different letters located at the beginning of a word.

Words beginning with /k/

cat	car
can	kite
kitten	key
cop	carpet
character	

Chart 3

Sounds that are made by one letter located anywhere in a word.

Words containing /b/

baseball	number
cab	rub
baby	football
box	cub

Chart 4

Sounds that are made by different letters located anywhere in a word.

Words containing /s/

sun	ice
circus	system
bicycle	bus
seal	himself

Chart 5

Sounds that are made by chunks of letters working together.

Words containing /or/

Oreo	score
horse	for
order	

NOTE: Focus sounds are featured in bold type.

Alphabet Book Activity

Most authors of alphabet books follow an unwritten rule when selecting words to represent different letters in the alphabet. For example, in *Kipper's A to Z: An Alphabet Adventure*, author Mike Inkpen uses nouns when introducing words that begin with a specific letter (e.g., "Aa is for ant. And Arnold"). However, rules are meant to be broken, and Inkpen breaks this pattern for the letters "N," "O," and "Q." Read an alphabet book to your students and challenge them to figure out the author's word selection rule. Then, see if they can find any instances in which the author breaks the rule.

Suggested Alphabet Books

Crosbie, Michael J. *Arches to Zigzags: An Architecture ABC*. New York: Harry N. Abrams, 2000.

Inkpen, Mick. *Kipper's A to Z: An Alphabet Adventure*. San Diego: Harcourt, 2000.

Martin, Bill J., and John Archambault. *Chicka Chicka Boom Boom*. New York: Simon and Schuster Books for Young Readers, 1989.

Pallotta, Jerry. *The Underwater Alphabet*. Watertown: Charlesbridge Pub., 1991.

—. *The Yucky Reptile Alphabet Book*. Watertown: Charlesbridge Pub., 1989.

song **6**

When the Rain Comes Down

"When the Rain Comes Down" is a peaceful, calming song that works well for morning-gathering or as a tranquil transition throughout the day. Students will also enjoy learning American Sign Language when singing this tune.

Lesson 6.1
Skill/Concept: American Sign Language (ASL)

Materials: CD set to track 6

Words to Sign

- "rain comes down"
- "everyone" (same sign as "us all")
- "no matter"
- "rich"
- "poor"
- "great"
- "small"
- "sun shines down"
- "flower blooms"
- "baby smiles"

- Children need to be familiar with the lyrics to "When the Rain Comes Down" before you introduce the ASL signs. Provide students with a brief overview of the function and uses of American Sign Language.

"When the Rain Comes Down"
© Bob Devlin, Moment in Time
Music, ASCAP, 1977

When the **rain comes down**,
It comes down on **everyone**.
When the **rain comes down**,
It comes down on **everyone**.
No matter if you're **rich** or **poor**,
No matter if you're **great** or **small**,
When the **rain comes down**,
It comes down on **us all**.

When the **sun shines down**,
It shines down on **everyone**.
When the **sun shines down**,
It shines down on **everyone**.
No matter if you're **rich** or **poor**,
No matter if you're **great** or **small**,
When the **sun shines down**,
It shines down on **us all**.

When a **flower blooms**,
It's blooming for **everyone**.
When a **flower blooms**,
It's blooming for **everyone**.
No matter if you're **rich** or **poor**,
No matter if you're **great** or **small**,
When a **flower blooms**,
It's blooming for **us all**.

When a **baby smiles**,
It's smiling for **everyone**.
When a **baby smiles**,
It's smiling for **everyone**.
No matter if you're **rich** or **poor**,
No matter if you're **great** or **small**,
When a **baby smiles**,
It's smiling for **us all**.

When the **rain comes down**,
It comes down on **everyone**.
When the **rain comes down**,
It comes down on **everyone**.
No matter if you're **rich** or **poor**,
No matter if you're **great** or **small**,
When the **rain comes down**,
It comes down on **us all**.

- List the words that students will be learning to sign on the board. Then demonstrate each sign, saying the word as you sign it. Have students say the word and practice signing with you. Then speak the song without the CD to help children learn the ASL signs. Now play "When the Rain Comes Down" as the students sing and sign along.

- Until students are fluent signing the words in the song, continue to review the ASL signs before playing "When the Rain Comes Down." As individual students become more skilled at signing, invite them to lead the class in singing and signing.

NOTE: Visit **www.maupinhouse.com** to see Cathy Fink and Marcy Marxer perform "When the Rain Comes Down" with ASL signs.

"Rain Comes Down"

Lift your hands up and to the right. Then bring your hands down in a right-to-left diagonal as you "sprinkle" your fingers like rain.

"Everyone"

Extend your arms in front of you at waist level, palms facing up. Then cross your hands and open them outward.

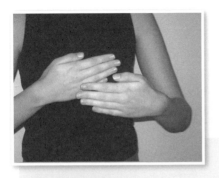

"No Matter"

Extend both arms out in front of you with your palms facing your stomach. Brush the back of one hand against the palm of the other twice, alternating hands.

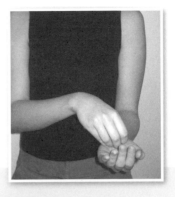

"Rich"

Extend your left arm in front of you at waist level with your left palm facing up. Cup your left hand and reach into it with your right hand as if you are pulling coins out of your left hand.

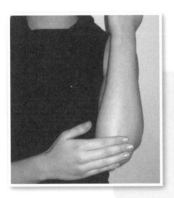

"Poor"

Bring your left hand up so it touches your left shoulder. Rub your left elbow with your right hand in a circular motion.

"Great"

Hold your arms out on either side of your waist, with your palms facing each other to indicate a large amount.

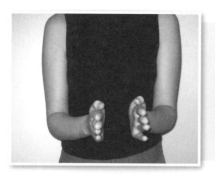

"Small"

Extend your arms out in front of you with your palms facing each other. Hold your hands a short distance apart to indicate a small amount.

"Sun shines down"

Draw a circle with your index finger over your head, and then with both arms spreading and dropping to your sides, let the rays of the sun shine down.

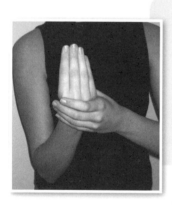

"Flower blooms"

Extend your left arm in front of you at waist level. With your left palm facing right, curl your left hand into a loose fist. Bring your right hand under your left. Push the fingers of your right hand through your left fist to simulate the petals of a flower blooming.

"Baby smiles"

Hold your arms as if you are cradling a baby. Then bring your hands up to your face, tracing a "smile" across your mouth with your fingers.

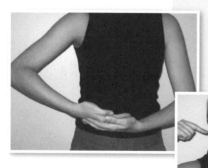
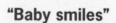

Lesson 6.2

Skill/Concept: Name Recognition, Letter/Sound Work

Materials:  CD set to track 6
▶ Student name card ring

- Prepare beforehand by writing each student's name on a 4" x 6" index card. Hole-punch the top left-hand corner of each card and hold them together with a metal ring. (This name card ring can be used again in Lesson 9.1 for the song "Goodnight, Goodnight" on page 34.)

- Play "When the Rain Comes Down" as the children come together for morning activities. Once the song finishes on the CD, sing the song again without the CD. Using the student name card ring, repeat the verse below until you zip in each child's name. For example:

    When <u>child's name</u> smiles
    He's/she's smiling for everyone…

- If your students already know the ASL signs, remind them to sign as they sing along.

- Learning names is a powerful way to teach children the relationship between letters and sounds. After you've greeted each student by singing their name, take a mini-teaching moment to review letter/sound relationships based on student names. For example, you might say, "Who can find the two letters that work together to make the /or/ sound in Corey's name? The /sh/ sound in Shawanda's name? Who can tell me another name that begins with the same sound as Jessica?"

Suggested Books

Bahan, Ben, and Joe Dannis. *Signs for Me: Basic Sign Vocabulary for Children, Parents & Teachers.* Berkeley: DawnSignPress, 1990.

Flodin, Mickey. *Signing is Fun.* New York: Berkley Pub. Group, 1995.

—. *Signing for Kids.* New York: Putnam Publishing, 1991.

A Ballet Dancing Truck Driver

One day my grandma asked me,
"What do you want to be?"
I thought and thought and
thought some more
I want to be a truck driver
(I want to be a truck driver).

But as I was watching TV
I thought ballet's the dance for me.
So now I know I want to be
A ballet dancing truck driver
(A ballet dancing truck driver).

Then I saw the Olympics,
So now I want to be
A runner racing—READY, SET, GO!
And a ballet dancing truck driver
(A ballet dancing truck driver).

Then we went to the circus,
So now I want to be
An elephant tamer—Sit here, please.
A runner racing—READY, SET, GO!
And a ballet dancing truck driver
(A ballet dancing truck driver).

Then we went to a restaurant,
So now I want to be
The finest cook—Soup's on!
An elephant tamer—Sit here, please.
A runner racing—READY, SET, GO!
And a ballet dancing truck driver
(A ballet dancing truck driver).

"A Ballet Dancing Truck Driver" presents a fun way to work on reading fluency with students and it serves as a good model for teaching intonation. Copy the picture cards on pages 44-47 to provide students with sequencing practice in independent learning centers and during reader's theater. Don't forget to consider this song for class performances!

Lesson 7.1
Skill/Concept: Listening, Sequencing, Fluency

Materials: CD set to track 7
► Class-made big book

Teaching students actions for each occupation in "A Ballet Dancing Truck Driver" integrates movement, listening, and sequencing into class performance. Use the actions listed below, or let your students create their own.

1. truck driver: grab an imaginary steering wheel and sing as you drive.
2. ballet dancing truck driver: turn in a circle on tip toes like a ballet step followed by truck driver motion.
3. runner racing: get arms into pre-race position and say "Ready, set, go!"

4. elephant tamer: make a large motion to show where the elephant should sit and say "Sit here, please."
5. finest cook: stir a large imaginary pot of soup and yell "Soup's On!"
6. carpenter nailing: pound an imaginary nail with an imaginary hammer and say "tap, tap, tap."
7. math teacher: use two fingers on each hand and say "2 and 2 is 4."
8. astronaut: put hands together, palms facing each other at chest level, raise hands over head, separate and say "Lift off!"

Once students are familiar with "A Ballet Dancing Truck Driver," create picture cards that illustrate the above actions (see pages 44-47) or those your students invent. Place the picture cards in a center for students to put in order, or keep props in the reader's theatre for sequencing and fluency practice.

Lesson 7.2  TARGET SKILLS™

Skill/Concept: Supporting Details, Onomatopoeia

Materials: CD set to track 7
► Chart paper

• Allow students to become familiar with "A Ballet Dancing Truck Driver" and then use this zipper song to work on expanding sentences with supporting details. After playing the song, pretend you're the grandmother, or zip in a new

I saw a new construction site,
So now I want to be
A carpenter nailing—tap, tap, tap.
The finest cook—Soup's on!
An elephant tamer—Sit here, please.
A runner racing—READY, SET, GO!
And a ballet dancing truck driver
(A ballet dancing truck driver).

But I really do love numbers,
So now I'd like to be
A math teacher—2 and 2 is 4.
A carpenter nailing—tap, tap, tap.
The finest cook—Soup's on!
An elephant tamer—Sit here, please.
A runner racing—READY, SET, GO!
And a ballet dancing truck driver
(A ballet dancing truck driver).

I looked up at the moon
And now I want to be
An astronaut—LIFT OFF!
A math teacher—2 and 2 is 4.
A carpenter nailing—tap, tap, tap.
The finest cook—Soup's on!
An elephant tamer—Sit here, please!
A runner racing—READY, SET, GO!
And a ballet dancing truck driver
(A ballet dancing truck driver).

One day my grandma asked me,
"What do you want to be?"
I said, "I don't know! There are so many interesting things to be!"
she said, "That's OK! You have plenty of time to decide.
And besides, you have lots of good ideas! Like . . ."

An astronaut—LIFT OFF!
A math teacher—2 and 2 is 4.
A carpenter nailing—tap, tap, tap.
The finest cook—Soup's on!
An elephant tamer—Sit here, please.
A runner racing—READY, SET, GO!
And a ballet dancing truck driver
(A ballet dancing truck driver).

character who asks your students what they want to be when they grow up.

- Write down each suggested occupation and corresponding supporting detail. Then zip in the new occupation as you sing the song. For example:

> Then we went to a <u>race track</u>
> So now I want to be
> A <u>race car driver – zoom, zoom, zoom!</u>
> And a ballet dancing truck driver
> (A ballet dancing truck driver)

- Each time the class adds another occupation to the list, ask one student to write out and illustrate the new verse. Compile these into a class book and make it available for repeated readings in both independent and shared reading activities.

Career Week Idea
Tell your students to choose careers they are interested in and zip them into "A Ballet Dancing Truck Driver." Then have students perform the reinvented song for your Career Week Assembly.

Suggested Books
Fox, Mem. *Sleepy Bears*. San Diego: Harcourt Brace, 1999.

Goodings, Lennie. *When You Grow Up*. New York: Phyllis Fogelman Books, 2001.

song **8**

It's a Shame

"It's a Shame" elicits giggles and grins from students as they learn the days of the week during daily calendar activities. But it would be a shame to limit "It's a Shame" to calendar activities. This song is also a fun zipper tune to use anytime during the day.

Lesson 8.1

Skill/Concept: Days of the Week, Listening

Materials: CD set to track 8
► Days of the week paper strips

- Before playing "It's a Shame," create seven strips of paper with a different day of the week written on each strip. Then select seven children to hold the paper strips, one child for each day of the week. If you teach younger children, line them up in order from Sunday to Saturday. Older students will enjoy placing themselves in the proper sequence. Their classmates can check to see if the days are in the correct order by signaling with a thumbs-up or a thumbs-down.

- To begin the lesson, instruct the seven students to hold their paper strips at chest level and raise them over their heads each time their day is sung.

"It's a Shame"
Traditional, new lyrics by Cathy Fink & Marcy Marxer, © Leading Role Music, ASCAP, 1984

It's a shame to get the
hiccups on a Sunday.
It's a shame to get the
hiccups on a Sunday.
When you've got Monday,
Tuesday, Wednesday, Thursday,
Friday, Saturday,
It's a shame to get the
hiccups on a Sunday.

It's a shame to lose your
shoes on a Sunday.
It's a shame to lose your
shoes on a Sunday.
When you've got Monday,
Tuesday, Wednesday, Thursday,
Friday, Saturday,
It's a shame to lose your
shoes on a Sunday.

It's a shame to wash the
dog on a Sunday.
It's a shame to wash the
dog on a Sunday.
When you've got Monday,
Tuesday, Wednesday, Thursday,
Friday, Saturday,
It's a shame to wash the
dog on a Sunday.

It's a shame to put a
pickle on a sundae.
It's a shame to put a
pickle on a sundae.
When you've got Monday,
Tuesday, Wednesday, Thursday,
Friday, Saturday,
It's a shame to put a
pickle on a sundae.

- Now play "It's a Shame" with all the children singing along. Students not holding a day of the week will enjoy acting out the song as they sing.
- After singing "It's a Shame" with the CD, sing just the chorus a cappella like the song "Bingo." There are two different ways to do this:

1. Once you make a day silent, keep it silent and then always sing Sunday in a dramatic way.

   When you've got (clap), Tuesday, Wednesday, Thursday, Friday, Saturday
   It's a shame to get the hiccups on a SUNDAY...

   When you've got (clap), (clap), Wednesday, Thursday, Friday, Saturday
   It's a shame to get the hiccups on a SUNDAY...

   When you've got (clap), (clap), (clap), (clap), (clap), (clap)
   It's a shame to get the hiccups on a SUNDAY!

2. Add a new challenge by leaving out one day at a time and clap in its place.

   When you've got (clap), Tuesday, Wednesday, Thursday, Friday, Saturday
   It's a shame to get the hiccups on a Sunday...

   When you've got Monday, (clap), Wednesday, Thursday, Friday, Saturday
   It's a shame to get the hiccups on a Sunday...

Lesson 8.2

Skill/Concept: Days of the Week, Daily Events

Materials:  CD set to track 8

- Play "It's a Shame," inviting your students to sing along.
- Now zip out *Sunday* and zip in the current day of the week. Have the children think of a school-related "shame" to zip in. Then sing without the CD, zipping in your new additions.

  For example:

  > It's a shame to <u>miss lunch</u> on a <u>Monday</u> (repeat 2X)
  > When you have Tuesday, Wednesday, Thursday, Friday, Saturday, Sunday
  > It's a shame to <u>miss lunch</u> on a <u>Monday</u>

  > Or

  > It's a shame to <u>lose your library book</u> on a <u>Tuesday</u> (repeat 2X)
  > When you have Wednesday, Thursday, Friday, Saturday, Sunday, Monday
  > It's a shame to <u>lose your library book</u> on a <u>Tuesday</u>

- The use of sundae/Sunday in the song can lead to a discussion of homophones (words that sound the same but have different meanings and usually different spellings) and homographs (words that are spelled the same but have different meanings).

Suggested Book
Carle, Eric. *Today is Monday*. New York: Philomel Books, 2001.

song **9**

"Goodnight, Goodnight"
© Cathy Fink, 2 Spoons Music,
ASCAP, 1991

When **Aaron** went to bed
and closed his eyes,
There were all sorts of
dreams to his surprise.
ONE little duck went walking by
And he waddled and he quacked and
he said goodbye.

When **Monika** went to bed and
closed her eyes,
There were all sorts of
dreams to her surprise.
TWO little lambs with
curly white wool
Pulled a ball of yarn
as far as they could pull.

When **Matty** went to bed and
closed his eyes,
There were all sorts of
dreams to his surprise.
THREE little kittens
purred and meowed,
And drank their milk
and took a bow.

When **Katie** went to bed
and closed her eyes,
There were all sorts of
dreams to her surprise.
FOUR spotted ponies
danced all night long
Playing guitars and
singing this song.

Goodnight, Goodnight

"Goodnight, Goodnight" invites children to visualize as they relax and it also links the creative, imaginative potential of dreams to narrative. Dreaming is also a good hook for students to hang new learning on, since it is a fun, whimsical concept for children. Consider using "Goodnight, Goodnight" as a transition song into independent reading by encouraging students to wonder out loud what images they will visualize after reading.

Lesson 9.1

Skill/Concept: Name Recognition, Counting,
Visualizing

Materials: 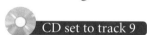 CD set to track 9
► Student name card ring

- Before the lesson, prepare a name card ring by writing each child's name on a hole-punched 4" x 6" index card and assembling all the cards on a metal ring. (You can use the same name card ring you prepared for Lesson 6.2, "When the Rain Comes Down," page 27.)
- Before playing "Goodnight, Goodnight," discuss dreaming and connect dreams to visualizing. Identify dreams as pictures we see in our minds while we are sleeping, and define the concept of visualizing as "awake-dreaming." Then,

play "Goodnight, Goodnight" for your students, asking them to note the kinds of pictures they "see" when they listen to the song.

- At the end of the song, ask volunteers to describe the pictures they imagined while singing "Goodnight, Goodnight."

- Now play "Goodnight, Goodnight" again, only this time hold up the name card ring and have students sing along, replacing the names on the CD with the names on the cards. Repeat the song until all students have enjoyed hearing their names sung.

- Young children can hold up their fingers and count from one to ten as they sing along with "Goodnight, Goodnight."

Lesson 9.2  TARGET SKILLS™

Skill/Concept: Descriptive Attributes, Rhyming Words, Alliteration, Strong Verbs

Materials: CD set to track 9
- ► Descriptive attribute chart
- ► Chart paper

- Review descriptive attributes with your class (see Appendix), reminding them that writers use descriptive attributes to help readers and listeners visualize. Ask students to listen for descriptive attributes as they sing "Goodnight, Goodnight."

- When the song is over, label and list all the descriptive attributes the children recall. For example:

When **David** went to bed
and closed his eyes,
There were all sorts of
dreams to his surprise.
FIVE furry fellows in
brown bear coats
Searched for their breakfast in
a box of oats.

When **Kyra** went to bed
and closed her eyes,
There were all sorts of
dreams to her surprise.
SIX silly seals were sliding down
A sliding board in the center of town.

When **Jared** went to bed
and closed his eyes,
There were all sorts of
dreams to his surprise.
SEVEN fuzzy baby chicks
Put on a show with magic tricks.

When **Sacha** went to bed
and closed her eyes,
There were all sorts of
dreams to her surprise.
EIGHT little mice
were squeaky clean
Eating cheese and drinking cream.

When **Michael** went to bed
and closed his eyes,
There were all sorts of
dreams to his surprise.
NINE baby bluebirds fell asleep
Until their mother brought them
something to eat.

When **Kelsey** went to bed
and closed her eyes,
There were all sorts of
dreams to her surprise.
TEN shooting stars all shining bright
Wrote in the sky goodnight,
goodnight.

Number: *one* duck, *two* lambs
Movement: *waddled*
Special feature (sound): *quacked, purred, meowed*
Texture: *furry*

- Challenge students to add more descriptive attributes to the list each time they sing the song. (There are at least thirty-five descriptive attributes used in "Goodnight, Goodnight.")
- Use "Goodnight, Goodnight" throughout the year, changing the listening focus from descriptive attributes to rhyming words, alliteration, or strong verbs. Also, since "Goodnight, Goodnight" is a zipper song, students can zip in different animals and attributes, names of family members and friends, or they can add additional verses to the end of the song and count beyond ten.

Suggested Books

Fox, Mem. *Time for Bed*. San Diego: Red Wagon Books/ Harcourt Brace, 1997.

Guarino, Deborah. *Is Your Mama a Llama?* New York: Scholastic, 1989.

Sendak, Maurice. *Where the Wild Things Are*. New York: Harper & Row, 1963.

song **10**

The Jazzy Three Bears

The rhyme, rhythm, and repetitive lyrics of "The Jazzy Three Bears" make learning fun while providing a natural scaffold to support retelling, fluency, and listening skills. This jazzed-up version of *Goldilocks and the Three Bears* offers a wide variety of activities for mini-teaching moments. You can create an easy literacy center extension by putting props, puppets, or costumes for "The Jazzy Three Bears" in your reader's theater or puppet theater.

Lesson 10.1
Skill/Concept: Listening, Retelling, Sequencing

Materials: 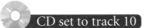 CD set to track 10
▶ Picture Cards (see pages 48-49)

- Play "The Jazzy Three Bears" as a warm-up activity for shared reading or read-aloud. Once students are familiar with the story, it's easy for them to speak in rhythm with the song. Think of actions they can do to represent different characters and objects in the story. Ask the children to snap their fingers to the rhythm of the words each time they hear the repetitive phrase "Be bop a be-bear, there was a little wee bear."

- Copy the picture cards of each character on pages 48-49. Then divide your students into three groups, one for each

"The Jazzy Three Bears"
Traditional, arrangement
adapted by Cathy Fink, © Leading Role
Music, ASCAP, 1984

Once upon a time in
a nursery rhyme
There were three bears,
I said three bears.

First there was the Papa bear,
Then there was the Mama bear.
Be bop a' be-bear,
there was a little wee bear.

They all went a walkin' through the green woods a talkin'.
Along came a little girl with long shiny golden curls.
Her name was Goldilocks, her name was Goldilocks.

She knocked on the door with a knock, knock, knock
And she walked right in 'cause there was no lock.

No one was there, no one was there.

She walked right in and
had herself a ball,
Just a eatin' and a rockin'
and a sleepin' and all.
She didn't care; no one was there
She didn't care.

Ho-ho-ho-home came
the three bears
Tired from the woods,
Ready to sit down to some home cooked goods, yeah.

CONTINUED

"Someone's been eatin' my
porridge," said the Papa bear.
"Someone has eaten my porridge,"
said the Mama bear.
"Be bop a be-bear," said
the little wee bear,
"In my bowl, there
ain't nothin' there."

"Someone's been sittin' in my chair,"
said the Papa bear.
"Someone's been sittin' in my chair,"
said the Mama bear.
"Be bop a be-bear," said
the little wee bear,
"Someone has broken my chair."

Well they went upstairs to
see what they could find,
They found Goldilocks in
bed asleep all the time.
She woke up, broke up the party
And boogied on out of there.

"Bye bye," said the Papa bear.
"Bye bye," said the Mama bear.
"Be bop a be-bear," said
the little wee bear,
"What kind of bear
is that there, huh?"

And that is the story
of the three bears,
I said the three, I said the three, I
said the three bears.

bear. One student from every group will hold up the bear's picture card as the other children in that group say the character's lines in unison.

- Once students know "The Jazzy Three Bears" well, try dropping your voice on several words or lines and let the children fill in the missing part from memory. It's good listening and retelling practice. For example:

"Once upon a time in a nursery rhyme
There were three _____,
I said three _____.

First there was the _____ bear,
Then there was the _____ bear.
Be bop a be-bear,
there was a little _____.
They all went a _____
through the _____ . . ."

Lesson 10.2

Skill/Concept: Fluency Practice

Materials:  CD set to track 10

► Class-made big book

- The students need to be familiar with "The Jazzy Three Bears" before working on this activity.
- Write the text of "The Jazzy Three Bears" on large sheets of construction paper, one paragraph per page. Then have the students create illustrations to match the text on each page. Bind the pages into a big book.
- Now chorally read the big book without the CD as a warm-up activity before a shared reading or read-aloud session.
- Place the big book in a listening center where students can work on fluency by reading "The Jazzy Three Bears" with or without the CD.

Suggested Books

Barton, Byron. *The Three Bears.* New York: Harper Collins, 1991.

Galdone, Paul. *The Three Bears.* New York: Seabury Press, 1972.

MacDonald, Alan. *Beware of the Bears!* Wilton: Tiger Tales, 2001.

"The Cowpoke Dance"
© Marcy Marxer, 2 Spoons Music,
ASCAP, 1986

The Cowpoke Dance

Chorus:
Ride'm high, ride'm low
Holler yippee-ti-yi-o!
Spur'em, fan'em, let 'em know
You're the champ of the rodeo!

I'm all dressed up and rarin' to go,
Rarin' to go to the rodeo.
You'll be there you buckaroo!
Oh my gosh, how I love you.

Chorus

Well, cowpokes come and cowpokes go
It's one dern thing I very well know.
To you, cowpoke, I'll e'er be true
Gosh, oh gosh, how I love you.

Chorus
Yodel

Clap three times!
Tap three times!
Snap three times!
Reach right over and touch your toes!

Everybody listening here,
Put your elbows in the air,
Put your hands up over your head
Shake your hands, then
shake your head.

Shake'em high! Shake 'em low!
Shake'em to the rodeo!
Put your fingers on your knees
And smile, so I can see your teeth!

"The Cowpoke Dance" works well any time
your students seem restless and need to
get up and move around. It's also a perfect
performance number for primary classes.

Bonus Lesson 11.1

Skill/Concept: Following Directions,
Directional Words and Phrases

Materials: 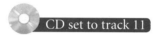 CD set to track 11

- Simply playing "The Cowpoke Dance"
  and inviting students to pretend they are
  cowboys or cowgirls will get them moving.

- After you have used "The Cowpoke
  Dance" a few times for movement,
  review some directional words and
  phrases before playing it again for a
  mini-lesson on directions. Then get up
  and dance the cowpoke!

Bonus Lesson 11.2

Skill/Concept: Listening, Comparisons

Materials:  **CD set to track 11**

▶ Pictures of a fiddle, banjo, and guitar

▶ Poster board, markers, yarn, scissors, glue

- First, play the "The Cowpoke Dance" for your class, asking students to listen for the different instruments that can be heard in the song. Allow students to name the instruments they heard in the song and list them on the chalkboard. Make sure the list includes fiddles, banjos, and guitars.

- After a brief discussion of all the instruments named, show students pictures of a fiddle, a banjo, and a guitar. Encourage them to identify the similarities and differences between the three instruments, making sure they notice the number of strings on each instrument (fiddle—four strings; banjo—five strings; guitar—six strings).

- Now provide children with the materials needed to make their own custom fiddles, banjos, or guitars. Students can draw instruments on poster board and cut them out with your help. Then, show them how to glue yarn onto the poster board cut-outs to create strings. When the instruments are completed, it's Cowpoke Time!

Clap three times!
Tap three times!
Snap three times!
Reach right over and
touch your toes!

Yodel

Put your left foot in the air,
Wave to your right foot a-way
down there.
Left foot forward, left foot back,
Tap your left toe, clickety-clack!

Hop on your right foot!
Hop! Hop! Hop!
Hop and hop and hop and stop.
Move your feet from side to side
Now you're doin' the pony ride.

Clap three times!
Tap three times!
Snap three times!
Reach right over and
touch your toes!

Yodel

NOTE: You and your students
will also hear the mandolin
and the stand-up bass in "The
Cowpoke Dance."

Appendix

Descriptive Attributes

Writers use descriptive attributes to help readers see in their minds, or visualize, what they are reading. Children need to be cognizant of descriptive attributes in order to improve their reading and writing skills. When students are aware of the descriptive attributes a writer is using to help them visualize, they increase their level of comprehension as readers and learn how to incorporate descriptive details into their own writing.

You can develop a student's ability to identify and use descriptive attributes by creating a class descriptive attribute chart or a big book based on examples students find in familiar literature and songs.

Select a few descriptive attributes to begin with, such as movement, number, and color. Continue adding new descriptive attributes throughout the year.

- **number:** four, one-half; *non-specific*: many, some, several; *comparative*: more than, fewer
- **movement or action:** gliding, slithering, flapping; *comparative*: faster, more frenzied
- **color:** purple, green, pale yellow; *comparative*: sea green
- **shape:** round, oval, cube, rectangular, columnar
- **size:** nine feet tall, ten yards; *comparative*: larger, as big as
- **location:** Eiffel Tower, bedroom, meadow
- **time:** sunset, dusk, daybreak, afternoon
- **direction:** left, right, up, down, backward, forward
- **texture:** smooth, bumpy, slippery; *comparative*: stickier
- **composition:** wooden, metal, plastic, glass, cardboard, paper
- **smell:** smoky, putrid, sweet; *comparative*: like smoke, muskier
- **taste:** sweet, salty, acidic; *comparative*: like licorice, fruitier
- **state:** liquid, solid, gaseous

- **temperature:** forty-six degrees; *non-specific*: boiling, freezing; *comparative*: hotter than, coldest
- **weight:** ten pounds, seven grams; *non-specific*: heavy, light; *comparative*: as heavy as, the lightest
- **age:** five years old, eighteen months old; *non-specific*: old, new, ancient, antique; *comparative*: older than Methuselah
- **symmetry:** horizontal, vertical, radial
- **special features:** striped, buttons, ribbed

(© 2003, Marcia S. Freeman, *CraftPlus*™)

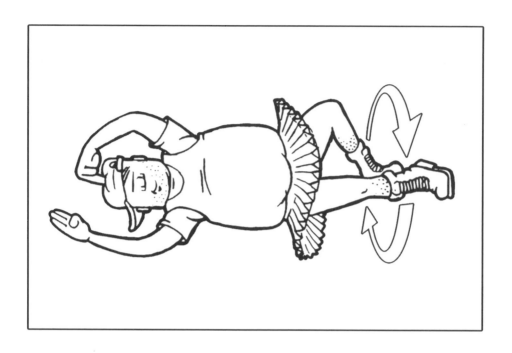

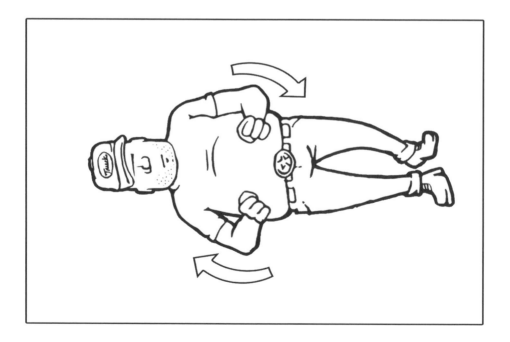

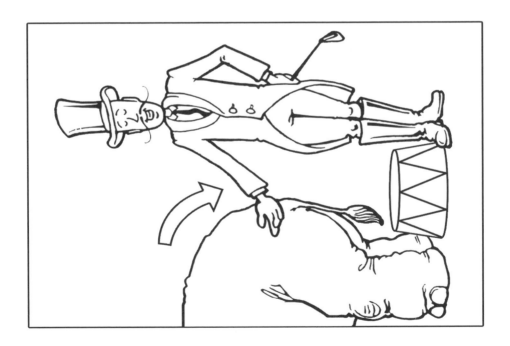

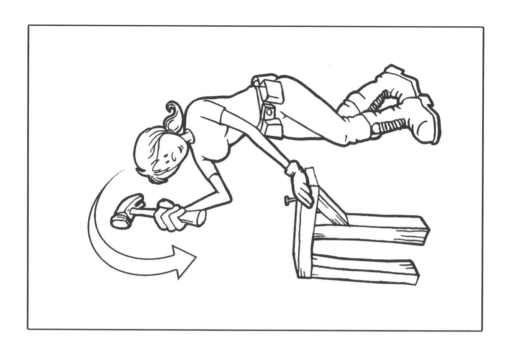

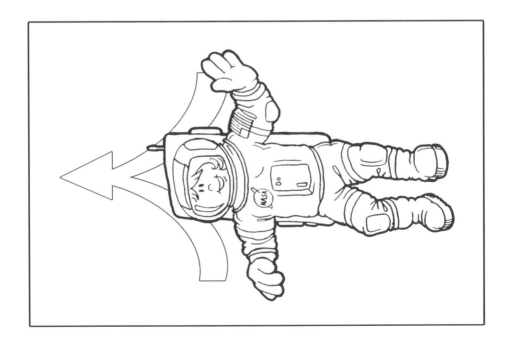

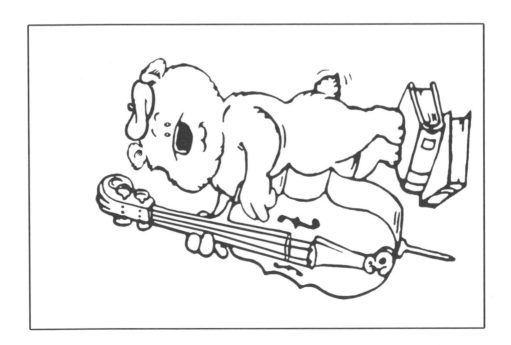

49

Bibliography

Brewer, Chris. *Music Memory Activities*. 5 April 2005.
   www.songsforteaching.com.

Cunningham, Patricia M. *Phonics They Use: Words for Reading and
   Writing*. New York: Longman, 2005.

Freeman, Marcia S. *Building a Writing Community*. Gainesville:
   Maupin House, 2003.

—. *CraftPlus Teacher's Guide*. Gainesville: Maupin House, 2004.

—. *Teaching the Youngest Writers*. Gainesville: Maupin House, 1998.

Jensen, Eric. *Arts with the Brain in Mind*. Alexandria: Association for
   Supervision and Curriculum Development, 2001.

Rasinski, Timothy V. *The Fluent Reader: Oral Reading Strategies for
   Building Word Recognition, Fluency, and Comprehension*. New York:
   Scholastic, 2003.

Wagstaff, Janiel. *Phonics That Work! New Strategies for the
   Reading/Writing Classroom*. New York: Scholastic, 1994.

Wood, Chip. *Yardsticks: Children in the Classroom Ages 4-14:
   A Resource for Parents and Teachers*. Greenfield: Northeast
   Foundation for Children, 1997.

About the Author

Luana K. Mitten graduated from Southern College in Tennessee with a BS in Elementary Education and received her MA in Reading Education from the University of South Florida. A former elementary school teacher and reading specialist for thirteen years, Luana currently enjoys the flexible schedule that writing and consulting work provide, allowing her to devote more time to her family.

Luana has written twelve non-fiction children's books and served as a literacy consultant for the Readers for Writer's series published by Rourke Classroom Resources. She is also the co-author of *Models for Teaching Writing-Craft Target Skills* (Maupin House, 2005).

As an education consultant and Head of Training for Maupin House Publishing, Luana works nationally with schools implementing craft-based writing instruction programs, modeling the use of non-fiction texts in reading and writing instruction, and teaching content through literacy. Raised by a teacher and the chair of a university music department, Luana understands the value of integrating music in the classroom. Her collaboration with Grammy®-winning songwriters Cathy Fink and Marcy Marxer, *20-in-10*, reflects her passion for encouraging learning through music.

About the Songwriters

Cathy Fink and Marcy Marxer are multiple Grammy® Award winners in the children's music field. They have been making music together since 1984 and have each been performing for over 30 years. Their recordings have also won numerous awards from the Parents' Choice Foundation, the National Association of Parenting Publications, the Oppenheim Toy Portfolio, and the Washington Area Music Association.

Cathy and Marcy have performed at the John F. Kennedy Center for the Performing Arts, the Philadelphia International Children's Festival, the Smithsonian Institution, The Today Show, The CBS Early Show, and on National Public Radio. Their children's music videos enjoyed rotation on the The Learning Channel for several years. Cathy and Marcy have presented keynotes, workshops, and concerts at conferences for the NAEYC (national and regional), the American Music Therapy Association, the Southern California Kindergarten Conference, the AFL-CIO, and hundreds of other organizations.

Empowering educators and parents to find more ways to include music in children's daily lives has been the centerpiece of Cathy and Marcy's success. Their live performances have set the standard for family participation and fun, while their recordings have inspired kids, parents, grandparents, teachers, and friends to sing together and enjoy the magic of music.

For a full catalog of books and recordings, write to:
Community Music, Inc.
PO Box 5778
Takoma Park, MD 20913
800-669-3942
www.cathymarcy.com